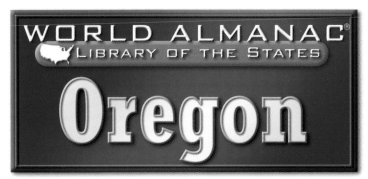

THE BEAVER STATE

by W. Scott Ingram

Curriculum Consultant: Jean Craven,
Director of Instructional Support,
Albuquerque, NM, Public Schools

WORLD ALMANAC® LIBRARY

Please visit our web site at: **www.worldalmanaclibrary.com**
For a free color catalog describing World Almanac® Library's
list of high-quality books and multimedia programs, call
1-800-848-2928 (USA) or 1-800-387-3178 (Canada).
World Almanac® Library's fax: (414) 332-3567.

Library of Congress Cataloging-in-Publication Data

Ingram, Scott (William Scott).
   Oregon, the Beaver State/ by W. Scott Ingram.
      p. cm. — (World Almanac Library of the states)
   Includes bibliographical references and index.
   Summary: Presents information on the history, people, geography, economy,
government, culture, and more of the state of Oregon.
    ISBN 0-8368-5143-9 (lib. bdg.)
    ISBN 0-8368-5313-X (softcover)
   1. Oregon—Juvenile literature. [1. Oregon.] I. Title. II. Series.
F876.3.I64   2002
979.5—dc21   2002022702

This edition first published in 2002 by
World Almanac® Library
330 West Olive Street, Suite 100
Milwaukee, WI 53212 USA

This edition © 2002 by World Almanac® Library.

Design and Editorial: Bill SMITH STUDIO Inc.
Editor: Kristen Behrens
Assistant Editors: Megan Elias and Gail Concannon
Art Director: Jay Jaffe
Photo Research: Sean Livingstone
World Almanac® Library Project Editor: Patricia Lantier
World Almanac® Library Editor: Monica Rausch
World Almanac® Library Production: Scott M. Krall, Tammy Gruenewald,
  Katherine A. Goedheer

Photo credits: p. 5 © PhotoDisc; p. 6 (clockwise) © Painet, © Classic PIO, © PhotoDisc;
p. 7 (top) © Corel, (bottom) © PhotoDisc, © PhotoDisc; p. 9 © PhotoDisc; p. 10 © Corel;
p. 11 © ArtToday; pp. 12–13 © Corel; p. 14 © Library of Congress; p. 15 © Corel; p. 17
© Library of Congress; pp. 18–19 © PhotoDisc; pp. 20-21 © Corel; p. 23 © PhotoDisc;
pp. 26–27 © Library of Congress; p. 27 © PhotoDisc; p. 29 © Corel; p. 31 (top to bottom)
© PhotoDisc, © Library of Congress, © Corel; p. 32 © Corel; p. 33 (all) © PhotoDisc;
pp. 34–36 © Corel; p. 37 © PhotoDisc; p. 39 (left) © Library of Congress, (right) © Dover
Publications; p. 40 (top) © PhotoDisc, (bottom) © PhotoDisc; p. 41 © Reuters/TimePix;
pp. 42–43 © Library of Congress; p. 44–45 © PhotoDisc

Printed in the United States of America

1 2 3 4 5 6 7 8 9 06 05 04 03 02

Oregon

Spirit of Independence

In the 1840s, Oregon came to symbolize a better future. The region, not yet a state, was the end point of a trail stretching from the Missouri River to the Pacific Coast. Many of the people who traveled the Oregon Trail were seeking their fortunes in gold mines. Others were leaving behind crowded towns and over-used farmland, hoping to start their lives anew in the open territory of the northwest. They crossed the continent in covered wagons, carrying only a few possessions, but they had faith that Oregon would provide for them once they arrived.

Oregon did provide for them, and for the many generations that followed. Dense forests and rich farmland abounded, yet Oregon offered more than economic resources. There were beautiful coastlines and breathtaking natural wonders, such as Crater Lake and Hells Canyon. Throughout the 1800s, Oregon's settlers established towns, built railroads, opened schools and libraries, and developed a distinct sense of identity.

Proud of their state's natural beauty, twentieth-century Oregonians became leaders in environmental protection, preserving their shorelines for the enjoyment of all and introducing some of the nation's first recycling laws. Fiercely independent, they also pioneered a system of state government that gives citizens more direct input when proposing and voting for new legislation. Oregon has produced some of the most innovative minds in U.S. history and culture. Scientist Linus Pauling, businessman Phil Knight, and cartoonist Matt Groening — all represent the originality of the state that has been drawing people away from the ordinary since Meriwether Lewis and William Clark first arrived on Oregon's Pacific Coast in 1805.

The Oregon spirit is the heritage of intrepid pioneers: men, women, and children who braved the rigors and dangers of the Oregon Trail to cross a continent and settle on land of their own.

▶ Map of Oregon showing the interstate highway system, as well as major cities and waterways.

▼ American explorers Meriwether Lewis and William Clark, along with their men, arrived at Cannon Beach, on Oregon's Pacific Coast, in 1805.

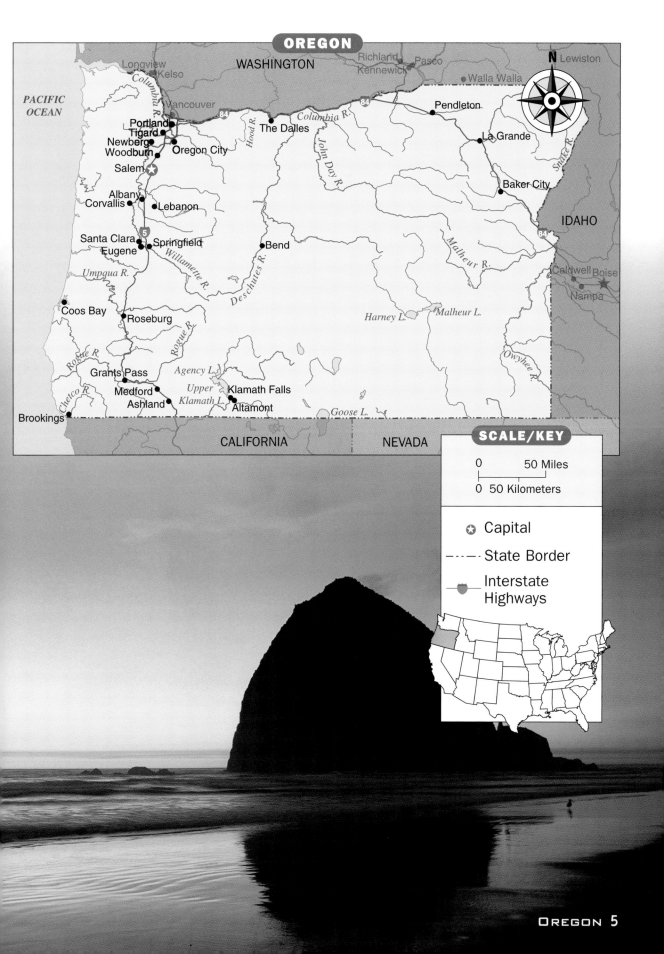

WASHINGTON

Longview
Kelso
Columbia R.
Vancouver

PACIFIC OCEAN

Portland
Tigard
Newberg
Woodburn
Oregon City
Salem

Albany
Corvallis
Lebanon

Santa Clara
Eugene
Springfield

Umpqua R.

Coos Bay

Roseburg

Rogue R.

Grants Pass

Medford
Ashland

Brookings

Chetco R.

Rogue R.

Willamette R.

Hood R.

The Dalles

Columbia R.

John Day R.

Deschutes R.

Bend

Richland
Kennewick
Pasco

Walla Walla

Pendleton

La Grande

Baker City

Snake R.

IDAHO

Caldwell Boise
Nampa

Malheur R.

Harney L. Malheur L.

Owyhee R.

Agency L.
Upper
Klamath L.
Klamath Falls
Altamont

Goose L.

N Lewiston

84

84

84

5

CALIFORNIA

NEVADA

SCALE/KEY

0   50 Miles

0 50 Kilometers

⭐ Capital

–··–··– State Border

Interstate Highways

Fast Facts

STATE OF OREGON

1859

OREGON (OR), The Beaver State

Entered Union

February 14, 1859 (33rd state)

Capital	Population
Salem	136,924

Total Population (2000)

3,421,399 (28th most populous state) — Between 1990 and 2000, population of Oregon increased 20.4 percent.

Largest Cities	Population
Portland	529,121
Eugene	137,893
Salem	136,924

Land Area

95,997 square miles (248,632 square kilometers) (10th largest state)

State Motto

Alis Volat Propiis — *Latin for* "She Flies with Her Own Wings."

State Song

"Oregon, My Oregon" *by J. A. Buchanan and Henry B. Murtagh, adopted in 1927.*

State Animal

Beaver — *Sometimes called "nature's engineer," this animal was the source of Oregon's early economic wealth. Beaver pelts were so valuable that they were among America's most hunted animals from the late 1500s to the late 1800s.*

State Bird

Western meadowlark — *The Oregon Audubon Society sponsored a poll of Oregon's schoolchildren, who chose the meadowlark as the state bird in 1927. Native to all of western North America, the meadowlark is known for the beauty of its song.*

State Fish

Chinook salmon

State Flower

Oregon grape — *Closely related to the barberry, this plant has small yellow flowers and, in fall, bears a small, dark-blue berry that can be used to make jelly.*

State Insect

Oregon swallowtail butterfly

State Tree

Douglas fir

State Gemstone

Oregon sunstone — *A semi-precious gem in the feldspar family, the polished stone ranges in color from clear to pinks, yellows, deep blues, and deep reds.*

State Beverage

Milk — *The state beverage is one of Oregon's most recent symbols. It was chosen in 1997 to honor the state's agricultural heritage.*

HOMOGENIZED MILK

PLACES TO VISIT

Japanese Garden, *Portland*

Designed in 1963 by Professor Takuma Tono of Tokyo, Portland's Japanese Garden contains five formal gardens in five different styles set on 5.5 acres (2 hectares). The gardens are acclaimed as some of the most authentic outside of Japan.

Oregon Coast Aquarium, *Newport*

Perhaps best-known as the aquarium that rehabilitated the injured orca (killer whale) Keiko, star of the 1993 film *Free Willy*, it was also the first to successfully breed harbor seals in captivity. The aquarium features nearly two hundred species of marine mammals, birds, and fish.

High Desert Museum, *Bend*

Since 1982, this highly regarded museum has educated visitors on the region's history, culture, arts, and wildlife. Exhibits include live animals in realistic habitats.

For other places and events, see p. 44.

BIGGEST, BEST, AND MOST

- Hells Canyon, along the Snake River, is the deepest gorge in the United States at up to 7,900 feet (2,408 meters) in depth.

- Crater Lake in southwestern Oregon is the deepest U.S. lake at 1,932 feet (589 m).

STATE FIRSTS

- **1915** The first swimsuit to be made of stretch fabric was developed by Carl Jantzen at the Portland Knitting Mills.

- **1938** The oldest pair of shoes — as old as nine thousand years old — was found in Fort Rock Cave in central Oregon. They were sandals made of sagebrush and bark.

- **1945** A Japanese incendiary balloon exploded in Lakeview, killing six people — the first civilian casualties during World War II within the continental United States.

What's in a Name?

In 1999, a Pennsylvania Internet startup, half.com, was looking for a way to publicize itself. It hit on an idea: Find a city willing to name itself after the company. In the year 2000, the town of Halfway, Oregon, agreed. For $75,000 and twenty-two computers, the town of 345 residents voted to unofficially rename the town half.com. The publicity worked; the move garnered half.com headlines across the country and landed the company's founder interviews with Katie Couric on NBC television's "The Today Show." The town of half.com used the $75,000 to buy a much-needed snowplow.

More Cones Than You Can Shake a Stick At

Southern Oregon has 10 million acres (4 million ha) of wild, rugged mountain country known as the Klamath-Siskiyou Bioregion. The World Wildlife Fund has identified the area as containing one of the most diverse conifer forests in the world, with thirty-five conifer varieties — more varieties than any other region of comparable size. The region also contains as many as 3,500 plant species, 280 of which are rare or grow only in this region. Conifers, or cone-bearing trees, include pine, spruce, and fir trees.

A Trail Through Centuries

> This is certainly a fertill and a handsom valley,
> at this time crouded with Native Americans. . . .
> we are all wet cold and disagreeable
> — *William Clark, U.S. explorer, 1805*

The first inhabitants of what would become Oregon migrated there as much as eleven thousand years ago. These first people settled along the coast, in the Willamette Valley, and on the Columbia Plateau. More than eighty tribes once lived in the Oregon region.

Among the people that settled in Oregon were the Chinook, the Yaquina, and the Tututni. They built permanent villages with wooden structures along the coast, where the climate was mild and seafood was abundant. The Klamath-Modoc tribe settled in the southern area of the state in the Cascade Range, living in earthen shelters in winter and portable teepees in summer. The Shoshone, Nez Percé, Walla Walla, and Yakima preferred the wide, flat lands of the Columbia Plateau. For shelter, they built tentlike structures called wickiups. They lived on bison, elk, deer, fish, roots, plants, nuts, and berries.

First Europeans

Spanish explorers were the first Europeans to sail along the Oregon coast as they searched for a Northwest Passage from the Pacific to the Atlantic. Oregon's rocky shores, and a thick fog, may have prevented English buccaneer Sir Francis Drake from landing in 1579. Exploration of the northwest coast was slow because of the difficulty of sailing around the tip of South America, which at that time was the fastest sea route from the eastern to the western coast of North America.

In the early 1770s, before the Revolutionary War, the discovery of a great river that flowed west opened Oregon to the first white traders. A U.S. trader, Captain Robert Gray, explored the river in 1792 and named it for his ship,

Native Americans of Oregon
Cayuse
Chinook
Clatsop
Coos Confederation
Coquille
Grand Ronde Confederation
Klamath-Modoc
Nez Percé
Shoshone
Siletz Confederation
Siuslaw
Tututni
Umatilla
Umpqua
Walla Walla
Warm Springs Confederation
Yakima
Yaquina

the *Columbia*. By fixing the river's latitude and longitude, Gray determined the width of the North American continent. Gray was also the first non-Native to set foot in Oregon.

Lewis and Clark

In 1803, the United States doubled in size when President Thomas Jefferson purchased the Louisiana Territory from Napoleon I, Emperor of France. In 1804, President Jefferson sent Captain Meriwether Lewis and Lieutenant William Clark on a mission to explore the Louisiana Territory. Starting from the trading post of Independence, Missouri, the party traveled up the Missouri River to the Rocky Mountains and across the rugged Northwest to the Pacific Ocean, guided by a young Shoshone woman named Sacagawea. Two years later, the Lewis and Clark party returned to its starting point and spread word about the great natural resources of the Northwest. Opportunities for fur trapping and trade drew Europeans, including British, French, and Russian traders, to Oregon.

Fur Trade and Settlement

In the early nineteenth century, beaver hats became so popular in the United States and Europe that the animals' fur became enormously valuable. U.S. trappers and traders were drawn to Oregon. Most followed the route marked by Lewis and Clark. In 1810, businessman John Jacob Astor

DID YOU KNOW?

Oregon's name may have come from the French word *ouragon*, meaning "storm" or "hurricane." The words *ouragon* and *ourigan*, however, were both used by English army officer Major John Roberts, who used the terms as early as 1765. He claimed they were Native American names for the Columbia River. Recent research suggests another possible source for the word. A highly prized fish oil called *ooligan* was widely traded by Native Americans. Their trade route ran through Oregon and along Oregon's rivers.

◄ Meriwether Lewis and William Clark canoed along the Columbia River in Oregon during their 1804-1806 exploration of the West.

formed his own fur-trading company, the Pacific Fur Company. He planned to set up trading posts from Missouri to Oregon. Attacks by Native Americans and the War of 1812 — between Great Britain and the United States — made the expansion of the Oregon territory fur trade difficult.

Even after the war, Britain did not want to give up its presence in Oregon. Most trappers and traders were English, French, or Canadian, and they traded with the world's largest fur company, Hudson's Bay Company. Fort Vancouver, a British settlement on the north side of the Columbia River in what is now Washington State, became the main trading post in the Northwest. To discourage U.S. competition (and settlement), the owners of Hudson's Bay trapped the beaver to near-extinction. Spain also claimed rights to the region but ceded its claim to the United States in the 1819 Adams-Onis Treaty.

The Movement West

The first U.S. trapper to reach Oregon overland was Jedediah Smith. In 1828, Smith and his party traveled north from California with a load of furs. The party was ambushed by Native Americans in the Willamette Valley. Smith's furs were stolen, but he managed to make his way to Fort Vancouver.

▼ The lush Willamette Valley.

The fort housed more than four hundred people within its stockade. Smith was able to recover the furs because the commander of the fort, Dr. John McLoughlin, had built strong relations with the Native Americans. Smith eventually left Oregon to trap elsewhere. McLoughlin became known as the "Father of Oregon."

Settlement Begins

By the late 1820s, the fur trade had declined because the beaver population had been almost wiped out. In addition, hats made from nutria fur and Chinese silk became fashionable. The young United States, however, continued to grow, and U.S. citizens pushed westward. In 1829, the American Society for Encouraging the Settlement of the Oregon Territory was organized in Boston, Massachusetts. The founder of the group, Hall Kelley, raised money and bought supplies to lead a party of settlers.

At the same time, a newspaper article claiming Native Americans in Oregon wanted to become Christians convinced two Methodist missionaries, Jason Lee and his nephew, Daniel, to join the Boston group heading to Oregon. In 1834 this new group of pioneers settled in the Willamette Valley near Oregon's present capital of Salem. Lee set up a mission. Although it was unsuccessful, the newcomers liked their new homeland. They sent word back East that this region of Oregon looked like eastern farmland.

By the late 1830s, fewer than one hundred white settlers lived in Oregon, but these few people had big ideas. At a meeting in 1838, the settlers wrote a petition to the U.S. Congress asking to be granted status as a U.S. Territory — the first step toward becoming a state.

Jason Lee rode east on horseback with the petition, speaking of the wonders of Oregon along the way. His more than seventy-five speeches found receptive audiences. The United States had fallen into a deep economic depression in the mid-1830s, and the promise of a new start in a distant and fertile land appealed to many.

Father of Oregon

Born in Quebec, John McLoughlin (1784–1857) became a doctor at age nineteen and joined the North West Company as a physician and fur trader. In 1821, the company merged with the Hudson's Bay Company, and McLoughlin was made a director. In 1825, he moved the company's headquarters to Fort Vancouver.

Under McLoughlin, Fort Vancouver became the largest trading center along the Columbia River, and he was widely respected by both whites and Native Americans. During McLoughlin's long tenure, there were no wars between the two groups. His charity toward travelers was also legendary — he fed weary arrivals and guided them to settled areas. His generosity to U.S. settlers, however, was not favored by his superiors at the British-owned Hudson's Bay Company, and they forced McLoughlin to resign in 1846.

McLoughlin then moved to Oregon City and became a surveyor and builder. He became a U.S. citizen in 1849 while serving as the city's mayor. Dr. John McLoughlin was named the "Father of Oregon" by the state legislature in 1957, one hundred years after his death.

Congress turned down the petition for territory status because there were not enough settlers in the vast region. So Lee decided to encourage more settlers by distributing copies of his speech. By 1840, the first wagon trains had gathered to make the journey to Oregon. The next decade saw hundreds of thousands of settlers make their way west.

The Oregon Trail

One of the main routes west — from Independence, Missouri, to Fort Vancouver — soon became known as the Oregon Trail. This 2,000-mile (3,200-km) journey had to be completed between spring and autumn before snow blocked the mountain passes. The first of the well-known "wagon trains" began the Great Migration in 1843 with a group of nearly one thousand people, more than one hundred wagons, and five thousand cattle.

The journey along the trail was harsh and perilous. Prairie schooners — the term used for covered wagons back then — did not have springs to cushion the journey. Bouncing wagons could cause loaded guns to go off. Anyone, young or old, could get sick from eating spoiled food or drinking dirty water.

On flat, dry land, a wagon train could travel 20 miles (32 km) a day. But in rough terrain, across wide rivers, or over mountains, wagons traveled much more slowly. Cooking was usually done over fires of dried bison dung called "chips" because trees were scarce. Although many

Packing the Wagon

Each wagon that traveled the Oregon Trail had to weigh less than 2,000 pounds (907 kilograms) or the oxen pulling it would work themselves to death. Supplies included easily preserved items such as flour, crackers, bacon, sugar, coffee, beans, and rice, as well as tools to repair the wagon and guns, shovels, and axes. These items plus clothing, bedding, and tents weighed as much as 1,800 pounds (816 kg) so there was little room for furniture, books, or family treasures. As more and more people traveled the Oregon Trail, it was not uncommon to see tables, bureaus, and other valuable — but heavy — items left at the trailside. Everyone except the very young and the very sick walked, instead of riding inside the wagon. Outfitting a basic prairie schooner cost between $600 and $800 — the equivalent of about $10,000 in 2002.

▼ A re-creation of the Oregon Trail.

popular stories told of Native American attacks along the route, relations between the settlers and Native Americans were initially peaceful. Some Native Americans acted as guides, while others were hired to help the wagon trains cross rivers or mountain ranges.

The Oregon Territory

Historians believe that about 10 percent of those who set out on the Oregon Trail died during the journey — as many as thirty thousand people. Nevertheless, by 1846, so many U.S. citizens had settled in Oregon that the British gave up their claim to the region. In 1848, President James Polk signed a bill creating the Oregon Territory. This territory included the present states of Oregon, Washington, and Idaho, as well as the western regions of Montana and Wyoming. In 1849, a territorial government was established in Oregon City, which lay along the Willamette River.

Thousands more settlers came to Oregon after gold was discovered in northern California in 1848. Once the news spread to the East, the numbers of newcomers exploded. Called the Forty-Niners after 1849 — the year that they arrived — most miners did not make a fortune in gold. They were encouraged to stay by the 1850 Oregon Donation Land Law. Any citizen could claim 320 acres (129 ha) of land, while a married couple could claim an additional 320 acres for the wife to hold "in her own right." To own the land outright, the claimants had to live on and farm the land for four years.

As was the case elsewhere, the arrival of newcomers had a disastrous effect on Native Americans. The land program, coupled with the settlers' diseases — smallpox, measles, and influenza — diminished the coastal tribe populations by as much as 50 percent. By the mid-1850s, most Willamette Valley Native Americans had been forced onto reservations. Wars broke out between the settlers and the Native Americans over the next twenty years.

Slavery and the Civil War

As the territory was settled by newcomers from the North and South, the question of slavery naturally arose. The decision as to whether Oregon should become a slave or free state was fiercely debated. Slavery was outlawed in 1844, but that did not mean that African Americans

DID YOU KNOW?

Historians believe that more than 300,000 people made the trip on the Oregon Trail from the 1840s to the 1860s. With so many traveling west along the same route, the trail became clearly marked and even today, in an area not far from Laramie, Wyoming, wagon-wheel ruts measuring 5 feet (1.5 m) deep can still be seen.

DID YOU KNOW?

The city of Portland grew so rapidly in the 1860s that when trees were cut down to make streets, there was no time to remove the stumps. The stumps were painted white so Portlanders could see to jump from stump to stump to make their way along muddy streets. As a result, one of the city's early nicknames was "Stumptown."

received equal treatment. Territorial lawmakers in Oregon passed the Exclusion Law of 1849, which banned all African Americans from the region. As a result, very few African Americans lived there when the territory entered the Union in 1859.

The bloody battles of the Civil War (1861–1865) occurred far from Oregon, but the war had a significant impact on the state's economy. With large herds of sheep in the Willamette Valley, Oregon became a major supplier of wool for blankets and other goods for Union troops. Agricultural products such as wheat also became major exports. Farmers, however, had trouble delivering goods to eastern states. Before the completion of the transcontinental railroad, goods from Oregon were transported overland by wagon train or by ships sailing around South America and up the eastern seaboard.

Railroads and Logging

The transcontinental railroad was completed in 1869. The western end of the line, however, ended in Sacramento, California. It was not until 1883 that a railway connected Portland to the East. The new ease of travel, and ease of trade, drew many immigrants to the state. During the last decades of the nineteenth century, logging became the major industry in Oregon. Thick forests of fir trees on the Coast Range and the Cascade Range became a valuable resource for the state and the country. Oregon soon became the nation's largest lumber producer.

▲ The 1910 *Chicago-Portland Special* sped people and goods from the East Coast to Oregon.

The Lash Law

One of the most notorious "exclusion laws" — laws intended to keep African Americans out of the Oregon Territory — was the 1844 "Lash Law." Under it, African Americans, slave or free, would be whipped twice a year until they "quit the territory." That law was amended six months later — African Americans would be required to perform forced labor. Repealed in 1845, the law was replaced in 1849 with a new law that simply banned all African Americans from settling in the region. Some African Americans, however, still quietly settled in the state.

The Twentieth Century and Beyond

Thanks to fertile farmland, abundant forests, and modern railroads, Oregon celebrated its fiftieth anniversary in 1909 with a healthy economy. The state's seventy-fifth anniversary in 1934, however, was not as bright. By the 1930s, the Great Depression had caused dramatic changes in the national economy.

In 1933, President Franklin D. Roosevelt developed a plan for economic recovery called the New Deal. This plan put jobless people to work building highways, irrigating desert areas, and developing recreational parks. The biggest project for Oregon was the building of the Bonneville Dam 40 miles (64 km) east of Portland. Thousands of workers labored on this project to harness the powerful current of the Columbia River. Once the dam was completed, electricity for homes and industries was available over an enormous area of the Northwest.

The electricity generated by the Bonneville Dam was so abundant that it helped make Portland one of the largest shipbuilding cities in the United States during World War II. The aluminum industry based in Portland also benefited from the growth of the shipbuilding industry.

During and after World War II, high-technology firms also established themselves in Oregon. This new industry, combined with the state's manufacturing base and natural resources, meant that Oregon's prosperity seemed assured. The state repudiated its checkered past by barring employment discrimination in 1949. The first African American to hold statewide office, however, did not do so until over forty years later. James A. Hill, Jr., was elected state treasurer in 1992.

Oregon also began to recognize that the state's wealth of natural resources was not inexhaustible. Conservation efforts started in 1967 when Oregon began to limit the amount of pollutants that companies could discharge into the Willamette River. Further groundbreaking conservation laws have followed.

Executive Order 9066

During World War II, Oregon participated in the relocation of Japanese Americans. Fearing that they would aid Japan, President Franklin Roosevelt ordered people of Japanese descent who lived along the West Coast to internment camps in several states, including Oregon. Many Japanese Americans spent the war years in these camps, forced to sell homes and businesses. In 1988, hoping to repair, at least symbolically, some of the damage, Congress awarded $20,000 to each surviving Japanese American who had been interned.

▼ Bonneville Dam turbines have been generating energy since 1938.

Oregonian Origins

> We have been burned out, flooded out, snowed under, and had hail storms that pounded the shingles off the roofs and broke every window in town. We have fought in every war and had a few of our own. Disaster comes fast and often but with each one we arise and go forward.
>
> — *Mrs. Ernest P. Truesdale, Canyon City, Oregon, 1939*

When Lewis and Clark arrived at the Oregon coast, the unexplored area was home to more than eighty Native American tribes that spoke thirty different languages. Although the Native people of Oregon had had little contact with Europeans, the diseases carried by explorers had already taken a terrible toll. By the 1840s, more than half of the original people of Oregon had become victims of disease and war.

The first wave of settlers that came to Oregon in the 1840s were U.S. citizens of English, German, and Scottish descent, who farmed in the Willamette Valley. In 1850, the first census taken reported the population of the territory to be 12,093. The population rose to more than fifty thousand by 1860, a growth rate of more than 400 percent.

Age Distribution in Oregon
(2000 Census)

0–4	223,005
5–19	720,999
20–24	230,406
25–44	997,269
45–64	811,543
65 and over	438,177

Across One Hundred Years

Oregon's three largest foreign-born groups for 1890 and 1990

1890 | 1990

Germany 12,475 | China 9,465 | Canada & Newfoundland 6,460

Mexico 28,913 | Canada 16,962 | Germany 8,139

Total state population: 313,767
Total foreign-born: 57,317 (18%)

Total state population: 2,842,321
Total foreign-born: 139,307 (5%)

Patterns of Immigration

The total number of people who immigrated to Oregon in 1998 was 5,909. Of that number, the largest immigrant groups were from Mexico (32%), China (7%), and Vietnam (6%).

Other Races, Other Cultures

It was not until after the Civil War that immigrants of non-European descent started settling in Oregon. In 1883, a coast-to-coast railway connection was established. The young men from China, Italy, and Greece who labored to build it worked during the warm weather and returned to their homelands during the winter. Some of these so-called "birds of passage" eventually decided to stay in Oregon and brought their families from their homelands. Large numbers of Chinese immigrants settled in Portland, as did immigrants from Italy and Greece. Jews fleeing anti-Semitic violence in eastern Europe settled in the Portland area in the late 1800s.

The arrival of the transcontinental railway brought African Americans to Oregon after the Civil War. Railroads were one of the few industries offering employment to minorities. Many African Americans worked as porters and conductors on the railways and thus did not live in

▲ Nez Percé and Yakima gathered in Astoria in 1911. Today, there are nine federally recognized Native American tribes in Oregon with more than twenty thousand members enrolled.

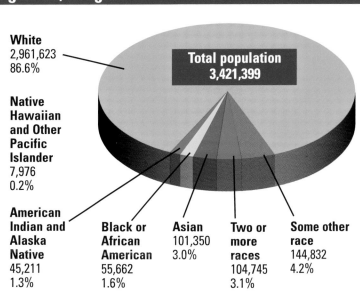

Heritage and Background, Oregon — Year 2000

▶ Here's a look at the racial backgrounds of Oregonians today. Oregon ranks forty-second among all U.S. states with regard to African Americans as a percentage of the population.

Total population 3,421,399

White
2,961,623
86.6%

Native Hawaiian and Other Pacific Islander
7,976
0.2%

American Indian and Alaska Native
45,211
1.3%

Black or African American
55,662
1.6%

Asian
101,350
3.0%

Two or more races
104,745
3.1%

Some other race
144,832
4.2%

Note: 8.0% (275,314) of the population identify themselves as **Hispanic** or **Latino,** a cultural designation that crosses racial lines. Hispanics and Latinos are counted in this category as well as the racial category of their choice.

the state on a permanent basis. The Exclusion Law that denied African Americans the right to live in Oregon was generally ignored with regard to the railway workers. Most African Americans who settled in Oregon communities were employed by hotels and restaurants that served travelers visiting the state. The last great wave of foreign immigrants occurred in the early 1900s, when Japanese immigrants arrived to work on small farms.

The population of Oregon grew more than 1,283 percent between 1860 and 1910 — from 52,456 to 672,765. The population continued to grow through much of the twentieth century, increasing by slightly more than 20 percent in the years between 1990 and 2000. The 2000 Census shows that the state has more than 3.4 million people. Less than half of the current population of Oregon was born in the state. People from other states and countries have been attracted to the state for many reasons. About 70 percent of the total population lives in urban areas. The median age of Oregon's

▼ The busy city of Portland is located where the Willamette and Columbia Rivers join.

Educational Levels of Oregon Workers (age 25 and over)	
Less than 9th grade	114,724
9th to 12th grade, no diploma	228,885
High school graduate, including equivalency	536,687
Some college, no degree or associate degree	592,902
Bachelor's degree	252,626
Graduate or professional degree	129,545

population is 36.4, higher than the 34.1 average of the surrounding western and mountain states, and also higher than the U.S. median average of 35.3.

Where They Live
Oregon has an overall population density of about 36 people per square mile (14 people per sq km), much lower than the national average of 80 people per square mile (31 people per sq km). This statistic is deceiving, however, because much of Oregon's enormous eastern Great Basin region is largely desert and thus sparsely populated. In fact, more than 70 percent of Oregonians live in the Willamette Valley, with more than half living in the greater metropolitan Portland area. Living space in the valley has become an important concern as the population continues to grow.

Religion
The first European settlers in Oregon were Protestant missionaries, and Christians of various denominations continue to make up the majority of religiously affiliated Oregonians. Among these denominations, Baptists, Lutherans, Methodists, and Presbyterians make up the largest group. Native American religions are still practiced by 1.4 percent of the population.

Education
The first schools in Oregon were founded by missionary organizations. The Oregon Institute, today Willamette University, was founded in 1842 and is the oldest college along the Pacific Coast. Lewis and Clark College, originally the Albany Collegiate Institute, was founded in Portland in 1867. The state's largest independent institution, the University of Portland, was founded in 1901.

There are twenty-six public and twenty-five private institutions of higher learning in the state. The state university system includes the University of Oregon as well as six other colleges and universities. Oregon also has seventeen two-year community colleges across the state.

▼ Villard Hall, on the campus of the University of Oregon, was named after Henry Villard, a strong proponent of public education, who gave the university considerable financial support in its early days. Today the building houses the theater department.

A State Made by Mountains

The first man to discover Chinook salmon in the Columbia caught 264 in a day and carried them across the river by walking on the backs of other fish. His greatest feat, however, was learning the Chinook jargon in 15 minutes from listening to Salmon talk.

— *from "Tall Tales and Legends" in* The WPA Guide to Oregon, *1940*

Oregon's beauty includes snowcapped mountains, valleys of rich farmland, and expansive forests. In the eastern region are high deserts and Hells Canyon, North America's deepest gorge. The spectacular scenery of the Columbia River and the views of the Pacific Ocean along the state's 296 miles (476 km) of coastline all add to the great natural beauty of the state. Major geological differences divide the state into five different regions. From west to east, these regions are the Oregon Coast, Willamette Valley, Cascade Range, High and Low Deserts, Columbia Plateau, and Great Basin.

Willamette Valley

Located between the Coast and Cascade Ranges, this valley is 115 miles (185 km) long and 30 miles (48 km) wide. More than 70 percent of Oregon's population lives here. Portland is one of the major shipping ports in the Northwest, mainly because of its location near the junction of the Willamette and Columbia Rivers. The mild climate and natural beauty make Portland one of the country's most livable cities.

Highest Point
Mount Hood
11,239 feet (3,426 m) above sea level

▼ *From left to right:* coastal view from Foulweather Point; Oregon Dunes National Recreation Area; Mount Hood; wildfowl in Shore Acres State Park; vineyards of Yamhill County, one of the world's finest wine-producing regions; elk at home in the Madison Grant Elk Refuge.

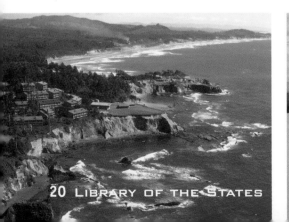

Coastal Oregon

Oregon's coast is an area of thick mists, steep canyons, and huge forests. Emptying into the ocean are rivers such as the Columbia, the Rogue, the Chetco, and the Gold. The rivers that cut through the Coast Range are a wilderness paradise for boaters, fishing enthusiasts, and nature lovers. Only one city in the region — Coos Bay — has more than ten thousand people, but the region draws millions of visitors every year. The residents of Oregon have always cherished their seashore and have passed laws limiting private ownership. All of the beaches are public land.

The Cascade Range

Mount Hood, the state's most recognizable landmark at 11,239 feet (3,426 m), towers over Portland. The mountain is part of the majestic Cascade Range that runs north–south along Oregon's entire length. The Cascades include several volcanoes, and in Oregon some are extinct and some inactive. One, Mount Jefferson, rises to 10,497 feet (3,199 m). The area features ski resorts, logging camps, and nature sanctuaries.

Crater Lake, Oregon's only national park, is a U.S. natural wonder. Located at the southern end of the Cascades, the lake was formed more than seven thousand years ago when the top of a volcano exploded. The surrounding glaciers filled the volcano's crater with water, forming the deepest lake in the United States with a maximum depth of 1,932 feet (589 m).

Desert Country and Plateau

To the east of the Cascade Range, in the central part of the state, are the high desert country in the northern central part and the low desert country in the southern central part. The Columbia Plateau, a terrain of rolling hills, lies

Average January temperature
Baker City: 25°F (-4°C)
Portland: 39.4°F (4°C)

Average July temperature
Baker City: 61°F (16°C)
Portland: 67.5°F (20°C)

Average yearly rainfall
Baker City:
 5.3 inches (13 cm)
Portland:
 37 inches (94 cm)

Average yearly snowfall
Baker City:
 26 inches (66 cm)
Portland:
 5.3 inches (14 cm)

Major Rivers

Columbia River
1,243 miles (2,000 km)

Snake River
1,038 miles (1,670 km)

Willamette River
309 miles (497 km)

John Day River
281 miles (452 km)

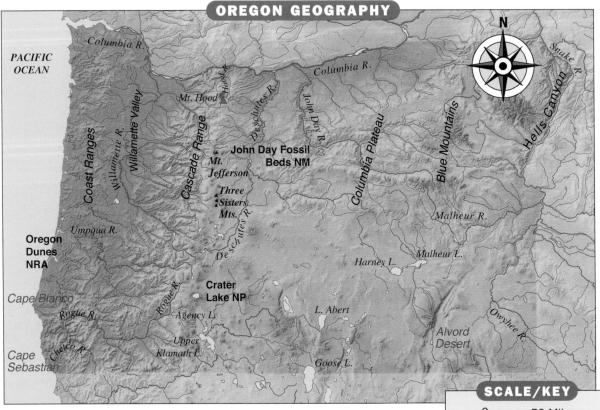

in the eastern section of the state. Cattle ranching once played a large part in the economy of the area. Wheat, wool, and lumber are the major industries today, but cowboys still rope, brand, and herd cattle as they have for generations. Every September in the town of Pendleton, cowhands from all over the United States and Canada take part in the nation's oldest and largest rodeo, the Pendleton Round-Up.

Great Basin

The Great Basin is a desert area in the southeast part of Oregon that makes up almost 25 percent of the state. Because of its dry climate, fewer than 1 percent of Oregon's population lives there. Ironically, one of the state's largest bodies of freshwater, Malheur Lake, is located in the northern part of the Great Basin. Its size varies, however, depending on the amount of rainfall. The lake may cover as much as 180,000 acres (72,846 ha) with shallow marshland water. At other times it is just a huge mudhole.

Climate

Oregon is a state divided by mountain ranges, so it has three distinctly different climates. West of the Cascade

Rose City, U.S.A.

The moist climate of the Willamette Valley is ideal for the cultivation of roses. In fact, Portland is nicknamed "The City of Roses" for the many rose bushes brought there by the first settlers.

Range, the climate is mild and moist. Precipitation along the coast can exceed 120 inches (305 cm) each year.

Much of the moisture in the west is trapped on the western slopes of the Cascades. East of the range, the climate of the Plateau and Great Basin areas varies from bitter cold to blistering heat. Eastern Oregon averages from 10 to 20 inches (25 to 50 cm) of precipitation each year. In the driest areas of the Great Basin, there is less than 10 inches (25 cm) of rain- and snowfall each year.

Plants and Animals

Forests cover more than 40 percent of Oregon's land. Among the more recognizable wildflowers of Oregon are the blue delphinium, Indian paintbrush, and glacier lily.

Oregon is home to a wide variety of wildlife, including North America's largest rodent, the beaver, as well as a high population of bald eagles. Larger animals include deer, elk, and antelope. Bears and cougars (also called mountain lions) are found in more remote mountain regions.

Two of Oregon's animals — the salmon and the spotted owl — have been the subject of great controversy. Dams and power plants on Oregon's rivers have destroyed the unobstructed waterways salmon need to reproduce. The logging of old growth forests has eliminated nesting areas of the spotted owl. Debates between environmentalists and industry have arisen over such issues.

Largest Lakes
Upper Klamath Lake 59,922 acres (24,250 ha)
Malheur Lake 49,000 acres (19,830 ha)
Lake Abert 36,670 acres (14,840 ha)

▼ Crater Lake is the deepest lake in the United States.

Making Money in Oregon

> We can reach our goals through an export-driven economy, public and private investment in education, infrastructure and social support, strong community partnerships based on outcomes, and a new vision for the natural resource sectors of our economy.
>
> — *"Oregon Shines II" 1997*

Oregon's economy has long been based on its natural resources. The first Europeans to travel to Oregon trapped native animals and traded their fur. Later settlers started farms in the Willamette Valley and produced cash crops such as wheat and dairy products. Oregonians exploited the state's dense forests as they developed a logging industry. Fishing and fish-processing also became an important industry as Oregonians made use of the salmon that crowded the state's rivers and streams. For most of the nineteenth century, Oregon industries struggled with the problems of transporting their goods to the rest of the nation, but twentieth-century innovations in road, air, and sea transportation eased these problems.

Manufacturing

The manufacture of cardboard, plywood, and other wood products once made up more than 60 percent of the manufacturing jobs in Oregon. Today, manufacturing jobs are spread across many industries.

High technology is the fastest-growing area of the state economy. Manufacturing companies in Oregon now produce software, electronic measurement devices, computers, and other electronic equipment. Portland and the Willamette Valley are where most high-tech companies are located. Service industry jobs make up the largest sector of employment. Workers in this sector include doctors, lawyers, waiters, and clerks, among others.

Top Employers (of workers age sixteen and over)
Services 32.1%
Wholesale and retail trade 22.9%
Manufacturing . 17.7%
Transportation, communications, and other public utilities 6.5%
Finance, insurance, and real estate 6.0%
Construction 5.6%
Agriculture, forestry, and fisheries 5.1%
Public Administration ... 4.1%
Mining 0.2%

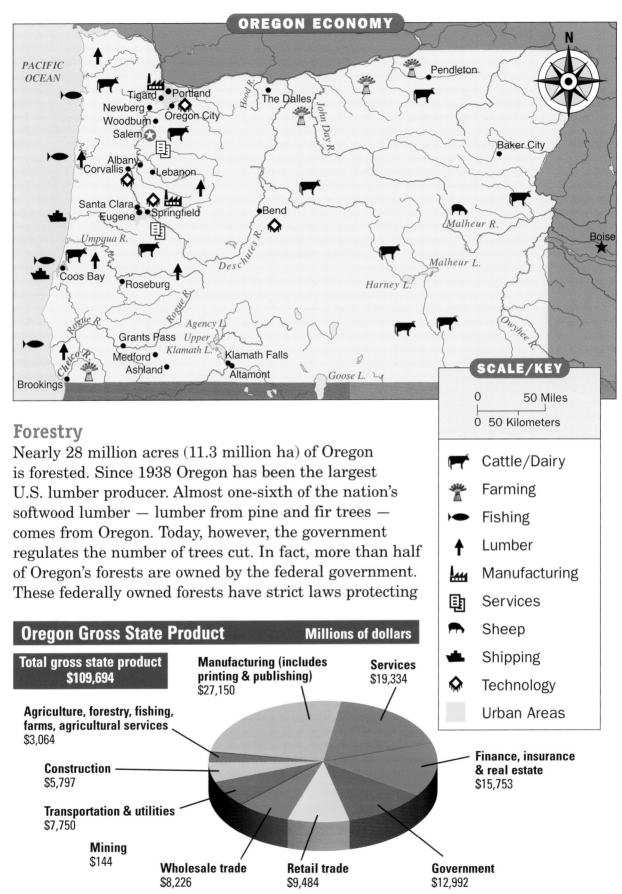

OREGON ECONOMY

PACIFIC OCEAN

Tigard • Portland
Newberg •
Woodburn •
Salem ☆
Albany
Corvallis • • Lebanon
Santa Clara •
Eugene • Springfield
Umpqua R.
Coos Bay
Roseburg
Rogue R.
Rogue R.
Grants Pass
Medford • Agency L.
Ashland • Upper
Klamath L.
Chetco R.
Brookings

Hood R.
The Dalles
John Day R.
Pendleton
Baker City
Bend
Deschutes R.
Malheur R.
Malheur L.
Harney L.
Klamath Falls
Altamont
Goose L.
Owyhee R.
Boise

SCALE/KEY

0   50 Miles

0   50 Kilometers

- Cattle/Dairy
- Farming
- Fishing
- Lumber
- Manufacturing
- Services
- Sheep
- Shipping
- Technology
- Urban Areas

Forestry

Nearly 28 million acres (11.3 million ha) of Oregon is forested. Since 1938 Oregon has been the largest U.S. lumber producer. Almost one-sixth of the nation's softwood lumber — lumber from pine and fir trees — comes from Oregon. Today, however, the government regulates the number of trees cut. In fact, more than half of Oregon's forests are owned by the federal government. These federally owned forests have strict laws protecting

Oregon Gross State Product   Millions of dollars

Total gross state product $109,694

Manufacturing (includes printing & publishing) $27,150

Services $19,334

Agriculture, forestry, fishing, farms, agricultural services $3,064

Construction $5,797

Transportation & utilities $7,750

Mining $144

Wholesale trade $8,226

Retail trade $9,484

Government $12,992

Finance, insurance & real estate $15,753

certain species such as the northern spotted owl, as well as strict antipollution and replanting requirements.

Agriculture

Sixty thousand people work on farms in Oregon. Counting those who work in the transportation, storage, and processing of farm goods, as well as those directly involved in farming, about 140,000 workers are employed in the agricultural sector.

Oregon's agriculture produces a wide range of crops. It is the nation's largest producer of Christmas trees, grass seed, hazelnuts, and blackberries. Plums, onions, cauliflower, and pears are also major crops. Oregon's more than two hundred agricultural products reach a wide market. More than 80 percent of Oregon's agricultural products are shipped out of state, including overseas destinations such as South Korea and Saudi Arabia.

The Willamette Valley, where the best farmland is located, is the state's most populous region. It has also experienced the largest population growth in the state over the last twenty years. As a result, large portions of farmland have been converted to industrial and residential use.

Water, like land, is another concern for the agricultural industry. Almost 50 percent of all Oregon farms depend on irrigation from rivers and streams. Those same waterways also support the commercial and recreational fishing industry. A growing population needing water and land limits the supply available to the agricultural industry.

Fish and Wildlife

The commercial and recreational pursuit of Oregon's abundant fish and wildlife bring in more than $1 billion each year. Small businesses, commercial fishers, charter-boat owners, tourist operators, and food processors are all

Twists and Turns

The Columbia River is the second-busiest river shipping system in the nation. Shipping goods along this river is not easy. The water's power can spin a 1,000-foot (305-m) supertanker around as if it were a toy.

All ships arriving or leaving Portland must have a specially-trained Columbia River pilot at the helm. As they move along the river, pilots may change course one hundred times during one trip. Fog can reduce visibility to zero, requiring the pilots to navigate the river without seeing the shoreline. The navigation channel is just 600 feet (183 m) wide. There's almost no room for error.

Captain Mitch Boyce, one of the only fifty Columbia River pilots, recommends: "The best way to pass another ship is to steer straight at it, then veer off at the last minute."

▼ Lumber has long been a major industry in Oregon.

part of this economic sector.

Commercial fishing was one of Oregon's first industries. The main catches, historically, have been Chinook and coho salmon. Years of overfishing, however, have led to a salmon shortage. Limits were placed on catches in order to help the Chinook salmon population grow, but the limits were eased as the population increased. The coho salmon, however, is close to becoming an endangered species. Snapper, sole, and whiting — Pacific bottom-dwelling "groundfish" — are now the main catch for commercial fishers. Between 1990 and 1996, harvests increased from 5 million to 155 million pounds (2.3 million to 70.3 million kg).

▲ Fishermen catch salmon by using gill nets or by trailing baited lines through water.

With more than 62,000 miles (99,758 km) of fishing streams and nearly 1,600 lakes and reservoirs, year-round fly and sport fishing play an important role in the state's economy. More than 600,000 fishing enthusiasts purchase fishing licenses each year. Hunting also provides recreational income for the state. Each year more than 300,000 hunters buy licenses and supplies from small businesses.

Made in Oregon

Leading farm products and crops
Greenhouse and
   nursery products
Beef cattle
Dairy products
Wheat

Other products
Wood products
Paper products
Electrical equipment
Machinery
Scientific instruments
Wool products

Major Airports		
Airport	**Location**	**Passengers per year (2000)**
Portland International	Portland	13,790,115
Rogue Valley International-Medford	Medford	492,065

Governing the Beaver State

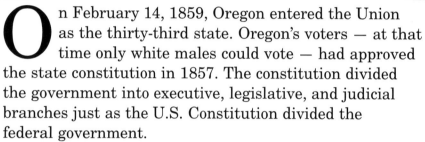

> The fact is, that these things that we cherish about Oregon have to be constantly renewed in ourselves and in our community.
>
> — *Oregon Governor John Kitzhaber, January 21, 2001*

O n February 14, 1859, Oregon entered the Union as the thirty-third state. Oregon's voters — at that time only white males could vote — had approved the state constitution in 1857. The constitution divided the government into executive, legislative, and judicial branches just as the U.S. Constitution divided the federal government.

Voting in Oregon is somewhat unusual in that votes are usually cast by mailing in a ballot rather than filling one out at a polling site on election day. Under Oregon law, voters may receive a ballot by mail on which they mark their vote. They must return the ballot via mail by election day. The use of vote-by-mail was first approved by the legislature in 1981, and in 1987 it was made a permanent feature of some elections. In 1998 Oregon voters amended the state constitution to require all primary and general elections held in May and November of even-numbered years to be conducted by mail. The 2000 primary and general national elections were conducted by mail.

The mail election is not the first time that the state of Oregon has been at the leading edge of politics. Early in the twentieth century, Oregon became the first state to pass a constitutional amendment that permitted laws to be passed by public initiative and referendum. Oregonians used this amendment to bring about a number of changes in their state. Oregon was among the first states to elect its U.S. senators directly rather than having them elected by state legislatures. The state was also among the first to give women the right to vote in 1912, and it was one of the first

The Oregon System

By the late 1800s Oregon's great natural wealth was controlled by a small number of powerful businessmen and state politicians.

William U'Ren, a soft-spoken but determined state representative, saw the corruption firsthand. He proposed an amendment to the state constitution that would allow initiative and referendum.

At the turn of the century, only elected representatives could propose laws. An initiative would allow voters to propose laws. A referendum allows citizens to vote on the legislation instead of permitting only elected officials to pass laws. In 1902 Oregon became the first state to pass a constitutional amendment allowing what is known as direct legislation.

Elected Posts in the Executive Branch		
Office	Length of Term	Term Limits
Governor	4 years	None
Secretary of State	4 years	None
State Treasurer	4 years	None
Attorney General	4 years	None
Commissioner of Labor and Industries	4 years	None
Superintendent of Public Instruction	4 years	None

states to initiate a presidential primary to determine voter preferences for their party's candidates.

In more recent years, the initiative process — called the Oregon System wherever it is used — has allowed voters to keep state lands from being developed and has created some of the strictest environmental laws in the nation. The system has also changed the taxation process that raised funds for education. Under an earlier system, education was funded by local property taxes. Some citizens felt that this system unfairly favored wealthy communities and needed to be made more equitable. In 1990 voters rejected property tax funding for education and chose to fund schools from other state tax revenues.

Executive Branch

This branch of the state government is headed by the governor. The governor and five other elected officials each manage a state agency or commission.

As the chief administrator of the executive branch, the governor serves on several state boards and is the chairman of the state land board on state land-use. Every two years the governor is responsible for submitting a budget to the legislature. The governor also signs into law or vetoes bills

▼ The state capitol in Salem was completed in 1938.

passed by the legislature. If the governor cannot complete a term, it is served by the secretary of state. In most other states the lieutenant governor would become the governor.

Legislative Branch

The Oregon legislature is the Legislative Assembly. It is composed of a senate with thirty members and a house of representatives with sixty members. Members of the Assembly propose and review new laws. A bill must be approved by members of both the house of representatives and the senate in order to become law. Once it has been approved by both houses, the governor may veto it, but this veto can be overruled by a vote of two-thirds of the members of both houses. Legislators also propose and vote on funding for new programs. Oregon has a citizen legislature, which means that legislators may hold other jobs. The legislature meets in January of odd-numbered years.

Judicial Branch

The seven justices of Oregon's Supreme Court are elected for six-year terms. It is the responsibility of the state judicial branch to interpret and rule on the legality of the actions taken by the legislature and the executive branch's state agencies. Oregon's Supreme Court also makes decisions on civil, criminal, and governing cases. The judicial branch below the supreme court is comprised of an appeals court, as well as circuit, district, county, and municipal courts.

Term Limits

Laws that limited the length of time state and legislative officials could hold office had been in place for ten years when the state supreme court overthrew them in February of 2002. Several bills were put before the legislature that would have reinstated the limits, but none passed. The legislature will meet for a special session in June 2002, and the issue of term limits will likely be raised again. Meanwhile a citizens group is sponsoring an initiative to place the term limit issue on the ballot in the state's November 2002 election.

DID YOU KNOW?

Oregon is the only state that has a different image on the reverse side of its state flag. One side shows the state seal and the other side shows the state animal, the beaver.

Legislative Assembly			
House	**Number of Members**	**Length of Term**	**Term Limits**
Senate	30 senators	4 years	None
House of Representatives	60 representatives	2 years	None

The White House via Oregon

HERBERT HOOVER (1929–1933)

Herbert Clark Hoover (1874–1964) was born in West Branch, Iowa. His parents died when he was young, and he went to live with his maternal uncle and aunt in Newberg, Oregon.

Hoover first drew widespread notice when he led major relief efforts during and after World War I to help the starving people of the Soviet Union. In 1921, President Warren G. Harding chose Hoover as secretary of commerce. He continued as secretary of commerce in the Coolidge Administration. When Coolidge chose not to run in 1928, Hoover received the Republican nomination for president.

The year Hoover became president, the 1929 stock market crash threw the country into an economic crisis. Hoover's Republican party wanted to let the business cycle run its course, but the president attempted several unsuccessful measures to stem the decline. As the Depression became worse, businesses collapsed and poverty grew. People began to blame Hoover for the calamity. The 1932 election brought a landslide victory for Franklin Roosevelt over Hoover.

An anticommunist and foe of international entanglements, Hoover denounced U.S. involvement in the Korean and Vietnam Wars. His last major activity was serving as chairman of the Hoover Commission, at the request of presidents Harry Truman and Dwight D. Eisenhower, which aimed to streamline the federal bureaucracy.

Local Government

Oregon is divided into thirty-six counties that, until 1958, operated as branches of the state government. Today nine counties have opted for home rule, which allows them to make their own laws within limits set by the state. The home rule counties and fifteen others are run by county commissions, which are administrative bodies composed of three to five members who are elected to four-year terms. The remaining twelve counties, which have smaller populations than the other twenty-four, are run by courts that consist of one judge and two commissioners.

▼ The Pioneer Courthouse in Portland was constructed between 1869 and 1873.

Having Fun in Oregon

> No quarreling, no improper language. . .
> no swearing. . . no dancing parties, no theatrical
> representations, no serenading of newly
> married persons, no bathing in the river on
> Sunday nor at any time without first having
> put on in private a decent bathing costume.
>
> — *from "The Rules to be Observed by All the*
> *Residents of Hopeland, Oregon" (no date)*

In a state as large and beautiful as Oregon, it is no surprise that there are lots of things to do and see. The fun isn't all outdoors, however. There are plenty of wonderful opportunities for indoor fun in the state as well.

Name a sport and you can participate in it — or watch it. Fishing, windsurfing, and clamming are a few of the activities people enjoy along the Pacific Coast. The state's largest rivers — the Columbia, the Snake, and the Willamette — draw thousands of windsurfers, rafters, jet skiers, and kayakers every year. Even big cities offer attractions for outdoor sports. For a number of years, Portland has been rated the top U.S. city for bicyclists by *Bicycling* magazine. The magazine rating is based on the city's downtown "Bike Central," which offers bike racks, showers, and lockers for a fee to anyone who wants to commute by bike to work. The city also has nearly 200 miles (322 km) of bicycle paths.

DID YOU KNOW?

The powerful winds created at the point where the Hood River flows into the deep gorge cut by the Columbia River create the best conditions for windsurfers anywhere on the West Coast.

▼ Windsurfing is one of the many sports residents and visitors can enjoy in Oregon.

For campers, hikers, and nature lovers, Oregon offers 13 national forests and 240 camping and recreational sites. The Cascade Range in the central area of the state is great for skiing in the winter and mountain biking in the summer.

One area that is a particular favorite of boaters is a region in the state's southwest corner, known as the "Banana Belt." Unlike most of the coast, which has a cool, moist climate, the Banana Belt is warm enough to grow tropical plants such as lemon trees and banana palms. The region, located on the Chetco River near the town of Brookings, is sheltered by a large peninsula of land that keeps away the constant cool winds from the north. The steep slope of the land also makes the mouth of the Chetco River one of the safest of the eleven boating harbors along the coast. For this reason it draws small boat owners who want to avoid the powerful Pacific surf. Not surprisingly, the Banana Belt is one of the fastest-growing areas of the state.

In the eastern high plateau region of Oregon, outdoor activities such as horseback riding, hunting, and fishing are extremely popular.

▲ Campers at Mount Jefferson are surrounded by Oregon's natural beauty.

Spectator Sports

Few if any professional teams have fans as loyal as those of the Portland Trail Blazers of the National Basketball Association (NBA). Oregon's newest professional team is the Portland Fire, which joined the Women's National Basketball Association in the 2000 season.

College sports also draw huge support from state fans. The athletic teams of the largest state universities, the University of Oregon in Eugene and Oregon State in Corvallis, have strong followings across the state. The football teams of both schools are annually

Sport	Team	Home
Basketball	Portland Trail Blazers	Rose Garden, Portland
Women's Basketball	Portland Fire	Rose Garden, Portland

among the top teams in the nation. Former University of Oregon football players Norm Van Brocklin and Dan Fouts are in the Pro Football Hall of Fame.

One of the most popular sports in Oregon colleges is track and field. The state has been home to a number of Olympic track athletes, including Alberto Salazar, Steve Prefontaine, and Mary Decker Slaney.

Performing Arts

There is also plenty to do in Oregon for those who don't participate in or follow sports. In the beautiful area of southern Oregon just north of the California border, two towns have popular summer festivals. From July through Labor Day, the town of Ashland hosts its annual Shakespeare festival. Work by the great English playwright and others is performed in a theater modeled after London's Globe Theater. Ashland is also home to nine different theater groups that present the works of various playwrights throughout the year.

About 15 miles (24 km) north of Ashland is the historic small town of Jacksonville. Each August, the town hosts the Peter Britt Music Festival, which is considered the foremost musical and performing arts event in the Northwest. The event draws musicians and singers in every style from folk to classical.

Jacksonville is also a tourist attraction due to its historic homes. During the 1850s, gold was discovered near the Rogue River, which runs through the town. The town was founded by miners and merchants and still retains the appearance of a frontier town. In 1966, the U.S. Department of the Interior designated Jacksonville a national historic landmark. More than eighty stores, mills, and homes are listed in the National Register of Historic Places. One of the most interesting of these places is the so-called Catalogue House. Built in 1893 by Jeremiah Nunan, it takes its name from the fact that Nunan ordered the house from a catalog as a Christmas gift for his wife. It was shipped west from Knoxville, Tennessee, in fourteen boxcars. Assembling the pieces took six months.

Oregon's desert areas provide fun for all-terrain vehicle riders. Skiers and snowboarders head for the hills.

The Cascade Mountains

These majestic mountains are the "picture postcard" of Oregon and the image most associated with the state. The most recognizable mountain in the chain is Mount Hood, which draws more hikers and climbers to its slopes than any other mountain in North America. As many as ten thousand people attempt to climb the mountain's summit every year.

In addition to Mount Hood, there are a number of extinct volcanoes in the Cascade Range that rise above 10,000 feet (3,048 m). There are few towns in

the range, but many people live there at various times of year. Ski areas, logging camps, and nature preserves bring thousands of people to the mountains. So many people have come, in fact, that in recent years the U.S. Forest Service has attempted to set limits on land use in many parts of the Cascades.

Places and Events in Eastern Oregon

The landscape and culture of eastern Oregon differ from that found on the western side of the state. The high plateau area retains a distinct flavor of the Wild West. Just outside the town of Bend, east of the Cascade Mountains, is the High Desert Museum, one of the most popular destinations in the state. The museum is dedicated to the environment, history, and culture of an area that comprises one-quarter of Oregon. There are scientific, Native American, literary, and historical displays throughout the museum. Walk-through dioramas depict realistic scenes of desert life. Outdoor exhibits include animals from the region — from birds of prey to porcupines. The museum is open year-round.

About 75 miles (120 km) northwest of Bend is the town of Pendleton. Famous for its huge annual rodeo, Pendleton

▼ Bison are the largest mammals native to North America.

also hosts an annual gathering of Native American tribes from the United States and Canada. Of all the town's attractions, however, one of the most fascinating places is underground. In the 1870s, Chinese immigrants arrived in the town to work on the transcontinental railroad. These laborers suffered from extreme anti-Chinese prejudice on the part of white settlers. Pendleton passed a law prohibiting Chinese immigrants from living in the town or owning property there. The Chinese immigrants got around that law by living *under* the town.

From the 1870s until the early 1900s, Chinese immigrants dug more than 70 miles (113 km) of tunnels under Pendleton. The "unwelcome" citizens created an entire community with living areas, stores, restaurants, and laundries. Today the original underground areas are open to visitors, and there are a number of modern stores and outlets in the famous "Pendleton Underground."

▲ Every year, Pendleton hosts one of the nation's best-known rodeos.

Visitors to Hells Canyon near Oregon's border with Idaho can see the animal that has grazed at the foot of the region's Blue Mountains for centuries. A herd of American bison, also called buffalo, are raised at the Hells Canyon Bison Ranch. The bison, the largest mammals in North America, are up to 10 feet (3 m) long and 6 feet (1.8 m) tall and weigh more than 1,000 pounds (454 kg). Bison are well-adapted for the region's cold weather, and their fur becomes thick and shaggy during winter months. The bison on the ranch are raised for their meat.

Famous Oregonians

> Do what you love, do it now. Start early.
> — *Ken Kesey, Oregonian author, 1999*

Following are only a few of the thousands of people who were born, died, or spent much of their lives in Oregon and made extraordinary contributions to the state and the nation.

MARCUS WHITMAN

BORN: *September 4, 1802, Rushville, NY*
DIED: *November 29, 1847, Waiilatpu, Oregon Territory*

NARCISSA WHITMAN

BORN: *March 14, 1808, Prattsburg, NY*
DIED: *November 29, 1847, Waiilatpu, Oregon Territory*

MISSIONARIES

Marcus Whitman studied medicine and received his degree in 1832. He practiced in Canada before returning to New York, where he became an elder of the Presbyterian Church. Narcissa Prentiss of Prattsburg, New York, had pledged her life to missionary work at the age of sixteen. In 1834, she married Marcus Whitman, and two years later the couple traveled to Oregon with another missionary couple, Henry and Eliza Spalding. Narcissa and Eliza were the first white women to cross the Rocky Mountains. The Whitmans reached the Walla Walla River and founded a mission among the Cayuse. In 1842, the Whitmans' church superiors in the East decided to close the mission because of a lack of converts. Marcus traveled through the winter to reach Boston and persuade them to reverse their decision. On his return trip in 1843, he guided the first "Great Migration" of eight hundred settlers to the Oregon Country. Soon, the Whitmans were ministering to the needs of the growing number of immigrants as well as to the Cayuse. In 1845, a measles epidemic struck both white and Native American children. Most white children recovered, but the Native American children, lacking immunity, died in large numbers.

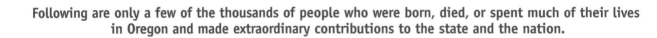

▲ The indictment against five Cayuse for the attack against the Whitmans.

Many Cayuse saw this as a plot designed to remove them. In November 1847, a group of Native Americans attacked, killing fourteen whites, including the Whitmans. They also kidnapped fifty-three women and children and burned the mission buildings. The attack led directly to the Cayuse War, which lasted until 1850. In that year five Cayuse were convicted of the Whitmans' murder and hanged in Oregon City.

ABIGAIL SCOTT DUNIWAY
WOMEN'S RIGHTS LEADER

BORN: *October 22, 1834, Groveland, IL*
DIED: *October 11, 1915, Portland*

Abigail Jane Scott was born in Illinois in 1834. When she was seventeen, Abigail's family settled near Lafayette, Oregon, where she began a career as a schoolteacher. One year later she married Benjamin C. Duniway. Four children followed. Duniway filled her days with child care and farm chores, but by 1859 she had found time to write her first novel, *Captain Gray's Company*. Her writing skills kept the family afloat when her husband suffered a crippling accident and, unable to work, lost the family's farm. In 1871 the family moved to Portland for a new start. At that time, the women's rights movement was active in Portland, and Duniway decided that a women's newspaper would provide income as well as an outlet for her writing. She founded the *New Northwest* newspaper during her first year in Portland. A newspaper devoted to politics, fiction, fashion, and domestic life, it was edited by Duniway for sixteen years. Duniway's reputation grew throughout the entire region, and she took many speaking engagements in the Northwest. National suffrage leaders called on her to serve as a vice president in the National Women's Suffrage Association in 1884. In her later years, Duniway led the Oregon Equal Suffrage Association. On November 30, 1912, Duniway signed Oregon's suffrage proclamation and became the first woman in her state to register to vote.

CHIEF JOSEPH
NATIVE AMERICAN CHIEF

BORN: *about 1840, Wallowa Valley, Oregon Territory*
DIED: *September 21, 1904, Colville Reservation*

Chief Joseph was born in what today is known as the Wallowa Valley. His tribal Nez Percé name was In-mah-too-yah-lat-lat, which means "Thunder Rolling in the Mountains." As an adult he came to be known as Young Joseph. Young Joseph became the leader of his people in the early 1870s, a time of increasing tension between the Nez Percé and white settlers. Young Joseph advised his people to keep peace with the settlers. His wisdom prevailed from 1871 to 1876. But in the summer of 1876, the first blood was spilled. In May 1877, Chief Joseph led his people to the Lapwai Reservation in Idaho, which was to be their

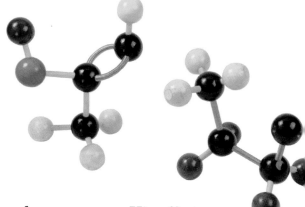

new home. The young warriors, however, were bitter. Along the way, three broke off from the band and killed four white settlers. Chief Joseph knew that the settlers would seek revenge and decided to lead his band to Canada. He took more than eight hundred of his people in that direction, pursued by U.S. Army general O. O. Howard. General Howard cornered the Nez Percé in Montana at Bear Paw Mountain, some 40 miles (64 km) from the Canadian border, in October 1877. Chief Joseph surrendered, issuing the legendary statement, "Hear me, my chiefs; my heart is sick and sad. From where the Sun now stands, I will fight no more forever."

LINUS PAULING
CHEMIST

BORN: *February 28, 1901, Portland*
DIED: *August, 19, 1994, Big Sur, California*

As a child, Linus Pauling lived in Condon, Oregon, where his father was a druggist. He later attended Washington High School in Portland and received his bachelor's degree from Oregon State College in 1922. From 1927 until 1964, Pauling was a professor at California Institute of Technology. For twenty-two of those years, he was chairman of the Division of Chemistry and Chemical Engineering, as well as director of the Gates and Crellin Laboratories of Chemistry. Over the years, Pauling also made advances related to the complex molecular structure of living tissue; sickle-cell anemia; a molecular model for explaining anesthesia; and vitamin C. He won a Nobel Prize for Chemistry in 1954. Beginning in the late 1940s, Pauling waged a campaign against war and

nuclear weapons. His efforts resulted in accusations that he was a communist, allegations that he categorically denied. In 1958, Pauling published *No More War!*, a book that called for abandoning not only further use and testing of nuclear weapons but also war itself. In 1962 the Nobel Committee announced that the Peace Prize was to be awarded to Linus Pauling. He is the only person to ever receive two unshared prizes.

BEVERLY CLEARY
AUTHOR

BORN: *April 12, 1916, McMinnville*

Beverly Atlee Bunn spent her early years on her father's farm in Yamhill until her family moved to Portland when she was six. She met her husband, Clarence Cleary, during her junior year in college. Before they married in 1940, Beverly studied library science at the University of Washington in Seattle and held the position of children's librarian in rural Yakima, Washington. Although she had wanted to write for children since childhood, she did not write for publication until she was in her early thirties. At that point, she wrote the children's book, *Henry Huggins*, which was accepted in 1950 by the first publisher who read it. Cleary has since written more than thirty books, with total sales of more than ten million. She has won numerous literary awards, including the Newbery. Her books include *Beezus and Ramona*, *The Mouse and the Motorcycle*, and her autobiography, *A Girl from Yamhill*.

PHIL KNIGHT
BUSINESSMAN

BORN: *February 24, 1938, Portland*

Philip H. Knight, a Portland native, attended the University of Oregon, where he starred on the track team. In the 1970s he got an idea for a new type of shoe while staring at a waffle iron. He poured liquid rubber into the waffle iron and created a running shoe that provided a better grip on running surfaces. This design became the Nike running shoe. By 1979, Nike, Inc. controlled 50 percent of the running shoe industry. In 1996, Nike, based in Beaverton, Oregon, had sales of more than $6.5 billion.

MATT GROENING
CARTOONIST

BORN: *February 15, 1954, Portland*

Matt Groening (rhymes with "raining") followed in his father's footsteps. His father, Homer, was a cartoonist. Growing up in Portland, Groening drew cartoons for his high school newspaper. In 1977 he moved to Los Angeles. Unhappy with his failure to find work, Groening decided

to create a comic book describing life in Los Angeles. Called *Life in Hell*, it soon became an underground success. In 1985 television producer James L. Brooks hired Groening to work on animated projects for his comedy series "The Tracey Ullman Show." To meet the request, Groening sketched a quirky-looking family of a father, a mother, two girls, and a boy. He named each character after one of his family members, except for the boy. He was named Bart, a play on the word "brat." This was the origin of "The Simpsons" animated television show on Fox Network. In 1990 "The Simpsons" debuted, earning both high ratings and critical praise. In 1997 the show became the longest-running prime-time animated show in history.

Oregon
History At-A-Glance

1579
Sir Francis Drake sails along the Oregon Coast.

1765
First written reference to "Ouragon" is made in Major John Roberts's petition to explore the American West.

1792
Captain Robert Gray explores the Columbia River.

1803
President Thomas Jefferson purchases the Louisiana Territory for the United States.

1805
Lewis and Clark arrive at the Columbia River.

1811
Fur trader John Jacob Astor founds Fort Astoria on the Columbia River.

1818
The United States and Britain agree that citizens of both nations can live in what is now Oregon.

1819
Spain gives up its claim to lands north of the 42nd parallel in the Adams-Onis Treaty.

1828
Jedediah Smith and company travel overland from California. Native Americans kill fifteen men on the Umpqua River.

1829
Dr. John McLoughlin establishes a claim at Willamette Falls, later Oregon City.

1834
Hall Kelley and a group of missionaries arrive in the Willamette Valley.

1844
Slavery becomes illegal in Oregon, and the Lash Law is passed.

1600   **1700**   **1800**

1492
Christopher Columbus comes to New World.

1607
Capt. John Smith and three ships land on Virginia coast and start first English settlement in New World — Jamestown.

1754–63
French and Indian War.

1773
Boston Tea Party.

1776
Declaration of Independence adopted July 4.

1777
Articles of Confederation adopted by Continental Congress.

1787
U.S. Constitution written.

1812–14
War of 1812.

United States
History At-A-Glance

1847
Marcus and Narcissa Whitman are killed in a massacre that leads to the Cayuse War.

1848
The Oregon Territory is created.

1850
The Oregon Donation Land Law goes into effect.

1859
Oregon becomes the thirty-third state on February 14.

1902
Voters amend constitution for initiative and referendum (the Oregon System).

1912
Women's suffrage is approved.

1938
Bonneville Dam is completed.

1945
Six Oregonians die in explosion of Japanese incendiary balloon.

1971
Nation's first Bottle Bill approved.

1991
First female governor, Barbara Roberts, is elected.

1992
First African American, James A. Hill, Jr., elected to state office.

1993
First statewide vote-by-mail election held in United States.

1800	1900	2000

1848
Gold discovered in California draws eighty thousand prospectors in the 1849 Gold Rush.

1861–65
Civil War.

1869
Transcontinental railroad completed.

1917–18
U.S. involvement in World War I.

1929
Stock market crash ushers in Great Depression.

1941–45
U.S. involvement in World War II.

1950–53
U.S. fights in the Korean War.

1964–73
U.S. involvement in Vietnam War.

2000
George W. Bush wins the closest presidential election in history.

2001
A terrorist attack, in which four hijacked airliners crash into New York City's World Trade Center, the Pentagon, and farmland in western Pennsylvania, leaves thousands dead or injured.

▼ Cowgirls at the Pendleton Round-Up, circa 1911.

Festivals and Fun for All

Check web site for exact date and directions.

Christmas Ship Parade, Portland

During the two weeks prior to Christmas, a parade of festive boats travels the Columbia and Willamette Rivers. The Christmas Ship Fleet is an all-volunteer group of approximately sixty boaters from the Portland/Vancouver area.
www.christmasships.org

Confederated Tribes Powwows, Pendleton

The Confederated Tribes (the Cayuse, Umatilla, and Walla Walla tribes) of the Umatilla Indian Reservation hold several powwows each year to celebrate native culture and traditions. Many of the gatherings feature drummers and dancers from all parts of the United States and Canada who compete in a number of different dances. The larger powwows include the Christmas Powwow in December, the Root Feast and Powwow in April, and the Wildhorse Powwow in July.
www.ohs.org/exhibitions/celebrate_powwows.htm

Dufur Threshing Bee, Dufur

Every year during the second weekend in August, visitors can step back in time to see the harvest being brought in with the help of horse-drawn equipment. This is the only threshing event in the Northwest that demonstrates every step of the harvest, from cutting standing wheat to sewing up bags for shipping.
For information, call: 541-467-2349

Fiesta Mexicana, Woodburn

Mexican Americans, one of the largest ethnic minorities in Oregon, celebrate their heritage. The event begins with the *Fiesta de los Niños* (Children's Day) and includes the crowning of the Fiesta Queen, as well as soccer tournaments and a candlelight procession, followed by a Mariachi Mass.
www.ohs.org/exhibitions/celebrate_fiesta.htm

High Desert Celtic Festival, Prineville

Celts (people of Scottish and Irish descent) have been a part of Oregon's history since the British Fur Company set up trading posts in the late 1700s. This festival celebrates Celtic culture with music, dance, food, and more.
www.ohs.org/exhibitions/celebrate_celtic.htm

Homowo Festival of African Arts, Portland

The largest cultural festival of its kind in the Pacific Northwest is a free, community-wide event that features African music and dance presentations, food, arts and crafts, storytelling, and workshops.
www.homowo.org

► A spectator at the Pendleton Round-Up calls, "Ride 'em, cowboy!"

► A spectator at the Pendleton Round-Up calls, "Ride 'em, cowboy!"

Oktoberfest, Mount Angel

The population of Mount Angel swells by a hundred times each September as the town celebrates its German roots with a traditional harvest festival. Dirndls and lederhosen — traditional Bavarian costumes — are worn by many performers and visitors.
www.oktoberfest.org

Oregon Dune Mushers Mail Run, Reedsport

Picture an arctic sled dog race — at the beach. Sled dogs pull wheeled carts 70 miles (113 km) along the Oregon coast from North Bend to Florence over two days.
www.harborside.com/~mjflcgs/odm

Oregon Shakespeare Festival, Ashland

From February to November, the festival produces eleven Shakespeare plays and other works.
www.orshakes.org

Oregon State Fair, Salem

For twelve days at the end of August, the Oregon state fairground becomes the fifth largest city in Oregon. Visitors consume more 250,000 hamburgers (20.8 tons of beef) and 833,333 hot dogs (78.9 miles/ 127 km laid end to end).
www.fair.state. or.us

Pendleton Round-Up, Pendleton

This annual event, held in September, features bareback riding, calf roping, steer roping, wild cow milking, wild horse racing, and many other cowboy sports. Native American dancing, parades, and several pageants are also part of the fun.
www.pendletonroundup.com

Pioneer Harvest, Oregon City

On the last weekend of November, the End of the Oregon Trail Interpretive Center in Oregon City hosts this event. Traditional harvest festival activities include making corn husk dolls, scarecrows, quilts, petroglyphs, and more.
www.endoftheoregontrail.org

Portland Rose Festival, Portland

The "city of roses" is host to a ninety-two-year-old tradition that attracts an estimated two million people each year to the Pacific Northwest.
www.rosefestival.org

Sandcastle Day, Cannon Beach

More than twenty thousand visitors watch about one thousand participants compete to build sandcastle sculptures within four hours.
www.cannonbeach.org/main/sandcastle.html

Books

Blackwood, Gary. *Life on the Oregon Trail*. San Diego, CA: Lucent Books, 1999. Read about some of the brave men and women who made their way across the continent to Oregon in its early days.

Cleary, Beverly. *A Girl from Yamhill*. New York: Dell Publishing, 1989. Popular children's author Cleary tells the story of her childhood in Oregon, from early days on a farm to life in the bustling city of Portland.

Gogol, Sarah. *A Mien Family Journey (Journey Between Two Worlds)*. Minneapolis, MN: Lerner Publications, 1997. Read the fascinating story of the Mien family, who emigrated from Laos to settle in Portland and start a new life.

Steedman, Scott. *A Frontier Fort on the Oregon Trail*. New York: Peter Bedrick Books, 1984. Find out what life was like for Oregon settlers in the nineteenth century.

Taylor, Marian. *Chief Joseph, Nez Perce Leader*. New York: Chelsea House Publishing, 1993. Learn more about this Nez Percé chief who led his people though difficult times in their history.

Web Sites

▶ Official state web site
www.oregon.gov

▶ Salem web site
www.open.org/~salem

▶ The Oregon Blue Book
www.bluebook.state.or.us

▶ The Oregon Historical Society
www.ohs.org

Films

Farrell, Michael. *In Search of the Oregon Trail*. Portland: Oregon Public Broadcasting/Nebraska ETV Network, 1996.